MY THOUGHTS
Through the Eyes of a Sinner

Kenneth A. Brown, Jr.

Copyright © 2016 by Kenneth A. Brown, Jr. All rights reserved. This book may not be reproduced or stored in whole or in part by any means without the written permission of the author except for brief quotations for the purpose of review.

ISBN: 978-1943258-62-8

Published by:

Charlotte, NC

Printed in the United States

I dedicate this book to my mother, Thelma Brown, and father, Kenneth Brown Sr., for their endless support and pushing me to pursue my passion. Also, thank you for encouraging me to press forward and trusting God regardless of circumstances and situations.

A DANGEROUS GAME

Crouched down, with my back against the bank,
I hide myself in my body armor and holding a gun to my chest,
My mind is boggled from the gun shots and explosions,
Praying that open fire doesn't meet my flesh,
My fellow soldiers have been fighting,
Fighting, losing blood, sweat, and tears,
Little did they know, fighting this battle was a test,
Because hundreds of us have lost many, many, years.

My prayers go out to their families…

But I just sit here on this bank,
Afraid to move because bullets are flying past my head,
Does this mean that I am not going to make it?
I never thought from joining this branch, I would end up dead,
An army of one,
When I entered, that's what I was told,
Do I put down my gun and grab my pen and pad,
So I can tell my story, the story of how my life unfolds.

What did I get myself into…?

NO!!! I am not going to be a coward,
I am going to face this war with open arms,
Stripping myself of my armor and protection,
And walk upright to face the storm,
After three steps, bullets ripped my flesh,
Then another parted my face,
OH MY GOD!!! What was I thinking?
This war just isn't safe.
Why did I do this…?

Now my face is to the clouds while taking my last short breaths,
Just wondering if I have time to gather a few thoughts,
Why did I play this dangerous game?
Not knowing along, my life has been lost,
I wish I could turn back the hands of time,
Wishing that in a safe place is where I would awake,
I pray that when I open my eyes, I see another day,
Because now I know this choice was a mistake…

I just hope it's not too late!!!

A TROUBLED MIND

I have spent many years worrying about my life,
And wondering whether or not I will succeed,
Constantly surrounded by put-downs and failures,
And believing that failure lives in me.

I have spent many years alone,
Not having someone to look up to,
Now I am afraid to travel the road of excellence,
Because my arms won't reach up to a high altitude.

I once heard there was no progress without struggle,
But should I experience so much pain and suffering?
My mind consistently boggled with distractions,
And stress that feels like death is coming.

It seems that all my contacts bring me pain,
So I continue expressing my life in between lines,
Letting procrastination alter my dreams,
Falling in love with distractions and gaining hatred with trying.

A troubled mind is all I know,
And my body is filled with stress,
Maybe one day this pain will be released,
And I hope there is success before I rest.

ASSIGNMENT

I once questioned the obstacles,
The lack of support, denials,
Almost broken from failures,
Too fatigued for trials.

But more trials came…
Along with more failures,
Searching new paths for hope,
No buried treasures.

So I embraced the struggle,
I welcomed the negativity,
Eyes opened by the beautiful lies,
The wickedness being in proximity.

In this chaotic environment,
I continue to strive,
Name being evil spoken of,
But I still smile.

What am I being prepared for,
Only the Lord knows,
Chapter by chapter the book unfolds,
Lick your fingers, take a scroll.

I have to stay strong,
Even if it's solitary confinement,
Keep grinding, no pages missing,
I have to fulfill my assignment.

BABY, I'M MISSING YOU

Baby, I'm missing you…

Higher than the sky,
Deeper than the ocean,
Further than east-west,
Nighttime dreams, morning devotion.

Baby, I'm missing you…

Your beautiful smile,
Heartfelt kisses,
Warming heart, tender kisses,
Comforting wings, just reminiscing.

Yes, it's very nostalgic,
But only for a short while,
Until my eyes meet yours again,
A breath of fresh air, deepest smiles.

Baby, I'm missing you…

Higher than the sky,
Deeper than the ocean,
The highest tides, deepest crest,
Angel wings, loving potions.

BEAUTIFUL LIES

Sometimes, I prefer to travel dark highways,
No street lights, no road markers,
No crescents for 72 hours… until,
Ms. Lunar powders her face.

No need to revive the moon,
Let's be entertained by the moments,
Motionless limbs, breathless lungs,
Be wakened by dreams, would you condone it?

Better yet… sleep beside the conscious,
Awaken beside the unconscious, turn veneer,
Take water to the floods,
Up drafts plus down drafts, intimate wind sheers.

Would you run towards the vortex?
A new American roulette,
Gambling away your soul, no balls,
And the casino not being present.

Are we going to interpret the picture being painted?
Lay in the bed with American induction,
Locking eyes with the beautiful lies,
Or lift a middle finger to the seduction.

BEAUTIFUL MUSIC

I love to hear the sound of your voice in the mornings,
It's like playing beautiful music,
The perfect melody, perfect tune,
A young man's dream, how do you do it.

Sometimes, I think you read my mind,
Like your words are only for me,
I try to surprise you with sweet nothings,
But you the say the exact thing, right before me.

Are you playing with my mind?
Making my heart lose control,
Am I on the Carbonaro Effect?
How did you kidnap my soul?

It's okay babe; you can keep it,
Please keep it forever long,
Your voice is beautiful music,
Just continue playing my song.

DEVIL'S PIE

I want you to know that I miss you,
Miss your pain, misery, frustration,
The emotional disagreements,
Intimate evacuations.

I miss your painful words,
The way that they pierce my heart,
Separating the body from the spirit,
Making toasts with evil counterparts.

We loved sipping wine with Devils' pie,
Having threesomes with nonbelievers,
Inhaling natures remedies,
While learning Lucifer's secrets.

His wands of wisdom being toxic,
And his words led to adultery,
My tongue manipulating your spirit,
My wands caressing your portrait.

Until next time my love…
As I await your beautiful presence,
Beautiful flames, tainted spirits,
The Devils' pie, my untold essence.

DIRTY MINDS

I want you so bad my love,
I cannot focus on my work,
Thinking about your smile, that walk,
I just love the way you work.

I just picture me entering the door,
Kissing, lifting that skirt,
And then you step away, saying come here,
Ooh, you are such a flirt.

I want you Michael Jackson bad,
Soft music, candles filling the air,
Deep kisses, rubbing your body,
Just to pause for a moment, look at you, the deepest stares.

I want to kiss all over your breasts,
Make my way down to your navel,
Slowly removing your Victoria's Secret,
Should we prepare the neighbors?

Never mind, let the world hear,
Lord knows what I want to do,
My tongue French kissing your center,
Juices down my face, loving the taste of you.

DISTILLED

I once heard that…
A double-minded man was unstable,
So I guess that I am a balance beam,
You and I were joined by the summer,
Holy matrimony, as the angels sing.

Education, grounded spiritually,
Nothing could be better it seems,
Largest bodies to powerful streams,
Within the closeness, we found friction,
And the waterfalls, to powerless streams.

Did the angels stop singing?
Did they disappear in the skies?
Darkest hours, thickest clouds,
Angels begin crying,
No tissue for the watery eyes.

Separate passions, separate dreams,
A new love separated by hills,
A love lost within the mountains,
Being stripped of its impurities,
So… I guess you can call it distilled.

So yes… a double mind,
Separate love, separate fears,
Separate prayers, separate nights,
We have lost substance, our stability,
No need for shallow tears.

GOOD BYE WINTER!

Stranger!! Reveal yourself!!
Climbing through my window, entering my home,
Dancing with my curtains, crackling the floor,
Please make your presence known.

Stranger!! Reveal yourself!!
Flickering my lights, tapping my phone,
Swaying trees, temperature falling,
Within the breeze you sing your weary song.

Stranger!! Reveal yourself!!
Hair standing, trembling in my bones,
Stay away, warmth come near,
Furnace breathe forever long.

Stranger!! Reveal yourself!!
No longer welcome, time to leave,
Falling backwards, must Spring forward,
Shadows be seen, set me free.

GOOD MORNING, MY LOVE

You arrive at consciousness,
Never late, always on time,
A breath of fresh air,
The sweetest flowers, sweetest pines.

Your presence is so warm,
Deep winter in front of the fireplace,
Hug me, kiss me, squeeze me,
Kiss my lips, caress my face.

You are the true meaning of warmth,
Never leave my heart, please stay warm,
It's so hazardous when you leave,
My personal unbearable storm.

The heaviness in my heart,
The happy tears in my eyes,
The shortness in my breath,
The small puddle from warm cries.

The anxiety in my heart,
The tingling in my bones,
The blood flowing through my vessels,
That makes my volcano erupt so strong.

You are the heaviness in my eyes,
My sweetest dream, my deepest phase,
Until its back to phase one,
The brightness, my sweetest rays.

Good morning, my LOVE.

HUNGER PAINS

Is this main course nourishment for the spirit?
Nourishing to my bones,
Enough nutrients to the body, tasteful,
No need for my fork to roam...

But yes! It roams!!

It roams to fill a void,
A need that has not been met,
So, I reach out to that side, the starch,
Because I need something to stick... no regrets.

But starch, understand your level of importance,
This amazing ride cannot be forced,
A different purpose, exotic moments,
But understand that you are not the main course.

Nourishing to my bones, my appetite is so heavy,
Starch I need you, this hunger, can you obtain?
My fork roams, it dances,
And then I have to report back to the main.

So yes! It roams!!

It roams to fill a void,
A need that requires fulfilling,
The main course released the Ghrelin,
So, I need you to provide the Leptin.

Please do not judge my hunger,
The way to a man's heart is to his belly,
Fulfill my passion, desires to my heart,
Stroke my emotions, you may add a veggie.

Now the veggie is for both of us,
More nutrients, personification,
Giving it life, make it sing,
Let's just call it additional decorations.

Exotic moments, yes exotic moments,
No main course, just my vegetarians,
Until the fork arrives, twisting emotions,
Becoming the equestrian.

Understand that you are my Leptin,
Don't get discouraged, know your role,
Quench my thirst, suppress my hunger,
Complete the course, until the napkin unfolds.

IMAGES

I was created in the image of Christ,
You were created in the image of me,
I am apart of him; you are apart of me,
So, I guess this is meant to be.

So many years I've longed for love,
I feel that I have searched every place,
I stopped searching and walked with God,
And then you appeared in front of my face.

I couldn't believe my eyes,
It would take too much to explain the logistics,
I prayed for you, and prayed for you,
And here you are down to the specifics.

Same family structure, same vision,
Same birth marks, same vision,
My desire to lead, your desire to follow,
Man… God has so much precision.

I have never experienced anything like this,
Never thought that I would be near it,
Being mesmerized by your personality,
Being infatuated with your spirit.

Oh my God, true beauty,
Everything that I prayed for was in you,
Love, intelligence, and determination,
I'm more than blessed to have you.

When I'm with you I feel at ease,
That's something I've never felt before,
Usually, I want space after so long,
But with you I want to spare more.

Time is very precious to me,
And you respected that without conflict,
That alone makes me want you,
Because for once, someone finally get it.

In my worst moments you bring peace,
Always pushing me, and making things better,
It's like you are my port during a storm,
Keeping me safe from the bad weather.
You encourage me more than ever,
Everyday I feel strong and confident,
You don't have an issue catering to your man,
Baby, I promise you are heaven sent.

HA HA! It's crazy how I need my sports time,
And you tune into my stations,
You please my mind, I please your heart,
So it's equal manipulation.

I remembered us watching the Bulls game,
And the game ran us out of our clothes,
But we had to stop because you are so special,
And I wanted to keep that door closed.

IMAGES-CONTINUED

In return, you said I was special,
So the feeling is mutual I suppose,
From that, you bought us both Bulls jerseys,
And you said that I was number one, not D Rose.

Baby you know the way to my heart,
I told God that this love is so real,
It's amazing how things come into your life,
Just from giving up a few meals.

Wow! This feeling is so amazing,
A thousand words couldn't explain this,
I have to hold onto you forever,
My sweetest joy, my sweetest kiss.

All I can say is this…

I was created in the image of Christ,
You were created in the image of me,
I am apart of him, you are apart of me,
So, I guess this is meant to be.

IN LOVE WITH MY PAIN

My mind is constantly racing,
Feeling that I'm experiencing mental confusion,
So, I vent and share my heart with you,
Allowing you to taste the illusion.

My mind is boggled from short-comings,
Having repetitive actions with the same results,
Flirting with sanity and insanity,
But…you are mesmerized by my approach.

Whispering in your ear with my misery,
Manipulating your mind with my frustration,
Taking your mind to new heights,
Before I release the vaccination.

Kissing you with my eyes,
Caressing you with my persuasion,
Fondling you with my swag,
Experiencing orgasms without penetration.

BUT… now you have been fooled by the confusion,
Wanting a spirit that is so strange,
You think that you fell in love with my heart,
But you really fell in love with my pain.

INEBRIATED

I need that alcohol edge,
That edge with no limitations,
No need to hold back, press forward,
A sense of arrogance, enhanced motivation.

I need that alcohol edge,
That edge without fears,
No need to worry, gotta have it,
Where you going girl, come here.

I need that alcohol edge,
That edge without a filter,
Regurgitated thoughts, just relax,
Systematic mind-set, raise the temperature.

I need that alcohol edge,
That edge with the finest purity,
Release the reality, no chase,
I might need security.

ISOLATION

C'mon people…

Why are we so afraid of being alone?
The need of having someone present,
Different passion, different dreams,
But you still search for the connection.

Ask yourself! What do I need,
Am I ready for an addition?
Multiple goals, multiple dreams,
OOPS! Sounds like a cloudy vision.

We must have a clear understanding,
Embrace the time, do not condone,
Growth occurs through duration,
But you learn plenty… from being alone.

LOVE ADDICTION

Baby! I am a junkie for your love,
I'm addicted to your presence,
Your love swept my shoes,
Falling for your essence.

When you are away...
My skin crawls for your love,
My feet constantly pacing,
Room to room, upstairs to downstairs,
Restless legs, instant palpitations.

Where are you my love?
Are you in the drawer?
Under the dresser, between the sheets,
Few options, pockets empty,
Should I just run the streets?

I need you my love...
I need you to roll back my sleeves,
Tie my arm with your love,
Inject your presence in my veins,
Five to ten seconds... I feel you my love...

Thank you baby!
Your presence is so appreciated,
Good feelings, emotional streams,
My world moving slowly,
My sweetest dream.

No! I am not insane!
But I feel withdrawal,
I need your presence, sweet kisses,
Joyful moments,
Just reminiscing.

Because I am a junkie for your love,
I'm addicted to your presence,
Your love just swept my shoes,
Falling for your essence.

MI AMOR

Water puddles fall from my closed eyes,
Rubbing my hair against the grain,
Having repetitive actions, expecting different,
But, I'm not insane.

Sniffles from my short nose,
Cotton crumbs on my fresh clothes,
Feelings on my sleeve,
No angel to wipe my tears, no.

Feeling hopeless, giving up dreams,
Life isn't what it seems, maybe,
Trying to rekindle the spark,
But, no wax have been dripping lately.

Just one question about my passion,
Wrap your arms around me with support,
This pad and pencil is not a sport,
Like a spirit needs the main course.

Cannot swim this river alone,
I need you love, did you forget?
Leave you ashore, I will regret,
Carried along to shipwreck.

Lost everything that's important,
Passion down stream,
Silent nights, deepest phase,
Absent from my dreams.

This toxic emotion is called love,
Not sent from above,
So, it must be returned,
No clear skies, with turtle doves.

All this pain, all of this time,
Wishing that we could press rewind,
Ponder on what went wrong,
Remove the needle, forget the song.

It's better to just move on.

MAYBE NEXT TIME

I am aware that I shouldn't have these thoughts,
But your beauty is beyond admiration,
Your intellect is second to none,
Voice beyond relaxation.

Sometimes in passing…
I'm thinking… why do you have to look this way,
Mesmerized by your physique, fair skin, long hair,
Wow! What should I say?

Maybe… could we go out sometime,
No, so crazy I want you in every way,
Wishing to kiss your lips, grab your hips,
But instead, good morning, have a nice day.

And then I peak over my left shoulder,
Wondering if you are peaking too,
Watching them hips twitch, oh my,
The things that I would do to you.

Maybe I should go fantasize,
About making love under waterfalls,
Water rushing, caressing your portrait,
You wrapped in my arms until nature calls.

Is it time that we meet again,
I'm prepared now, let's press rewind,
Star struck by your presence,
With smiles… have a good day… maybe next time

MY ANGEL

Sometimes, I would have some painful days,
Days that would leave my mind boggled and confused,
And all I could do was just sit and wonder,
Just scared if my prayers would come through.

It didn't matter what battle I was facing,
My mind would always be cluttered with fear,
My eyes would stream with me feeling helpless,
Until this angel came and wiped my tears.

I knew that I shouldn't be discouraged,
And for my goals I needed to strive,
Along the way I felt loved and confident,
Because I knew that angel was by my side.

My success was just a few breaths away,
But for some reason I had this doubt in my mind,
I had asked myself "why do I feel this way?"
Then that angel said, "I would be just fine."

Now I know my prayers have been answered,
Because all of my dreams are coming true,
I thank God for having you in my life,
Knowing that angel by my side is you.

Thanks Mom

MIRRORS

As a kid, I remember looking in the mirror,
Asking myself, what does this man embody?
Are my talents going to be utilized?
Or just environmental hobbies.

Because all of my friends were lost,
Searching for keys to locked doors,
Wondering the streets without fathers,
And the streets poison exiting our pores.

We couldn't see reflections,
Wasting energy at street corners,
Watching our fathers get high,
Selling souls into the morning.

So I walked around empty,
And blaming everyone for my problems,
No one to give me guidance,
Having no means of solving them.

I forced myself to become educated,
Living my dreams between lines,
Pushing my passion across paper,
A new high, longer than 20 minutes, pass the time.

So I cried, and cried,
Asking God to reveal himself,
Praying for wisdom and guidance,
I needed to save myself, from myself.

Everything that I touched turned golden,
And all of my pathways became paved,
I sacrificed my fleshly ways,
And watched my father get saved.

So I moved… continued to move,
Searching for more without questions,
More money, new clothes, enlarged territory,
Overwhelmed with blessings.

And then my father changed,
God you are so awesome,
My father and I submitted to you,
Belonging, no more lost ones.

Conquering more than imagined,
Barriers broken by streams,
Windows opened with singing Angels,
A father's love, living beyond my dreams.

It's amazing how things change,
My father and I achieved even more,
Father God you told me to trust you,
And all of these years have been restored.

So, now I have unlocked new doors,
And my talents have reached perfection,
Looking in the mirrors with confidence,
Finally seeing Kenneth Sr's reflection.

Man, I'm so awesome!

MY SWEET IRISH ROSE

I believe I fell in you face first,
Suffocating with my head spinning,
I have to escape all this bickering,
Man… 'Cause you be trippin'.

First, you said "I never want to chill with you,"
But all we do is fuss,
Then you said "every relationship has ups and downs,"
So I guess the stress is a must.

Fuss about the quality time,
Fuss about me going to the bar,
Shoulda warmed my heart with someone else,
So my mind can travel far.

This way I can have some kind of peace.

But then you'll be that cloudy image on my shoulder,
Just screaming in my ear,
Oh God! My body is tingling,
Lord… is you finally here?

You feel my belly with warmth,
Take all my money,
The only time we don't argue is when my lips touch…
Oops!
Isn't that funny.

But you coulda kept the warmth,
And I coulda kept my money,
You get pissed off and rub everything in my face,
Now I feel like the dummy.

The loving is good it sure is,
But is it worth all this pain?
Maybe I should just leave you,
But I love the way you say my name.

Man, I'm in too deep.

Why do you do this my Irish rose?
Just one more taste and I'll leave you be,
Oh no! What is this mess?
Just smelling all over me.

Did I do this again?
Yep! That's what it seems,
I thought I had some crazy woman blues,
But I guess it was all a dream.

Man!!!! Need to stop drinking.

NO OTHER LOVE

It's only been moments since we made love,
Fast asleep you go…
Love in the air,
The sweet smell of French Vanilla candles,
Intertwined with our love,
A new fragrance, my love can bare.

My fair skin angel…
You are so beautiful my love,
Face so soft,
Lips so sweet from deep kisses,
One mind, one spirit,
One more kiss my love…

Are you having sweet dreams?
You are sleeping so peacefully,
Shallow breaths,
Your soft song playing,
Chest rising, wings moving,
Mesmerized by your Victoria's Secret…

You asked me does love feel like this?
I don't know my love,
My feelings for you are unexplainable,
So soothing, so peaceful,
Loving you is so precious,
I don't want another feeling.

REARVIEW MIRRORS

Sometimes I would pray for warm summers,
Beautiful flowers, green grass,
Stop and go traffic… be patient,
No worries please… avoid the crash.

Not a physical crash,
But maybe metaphorically,
Just like seeing is believing,
Abrupt interruptions, oratorically.

Mistakes becoming failures,
Love becoming a lust,
It all goes hand in hand,
So the transaction is a must.

But are summers really peaceful?
All of the egregious activity,
Selling hopes to steal dreams,
Enjoying the corrupted activities.

Are you feeling blessed to feel summer,
Beautiful flowers, clear skies,
Street corners to churches,
Gunplay as the angel cries.

Let's jump in the car!
By pass the flowers, and clear skies,
Atrocious interaction when the sun sets,
Until the rearview mirror show sunrise.

ON THE WEEKENDS...

I like to get up bright and early,
Go to stores, wait in lines,
See people stare, looking at my attire,
I'm not what they have in mind.

They see the ears pierced,
Fresh cut, yes, the high and tight,
Waves spinning, tee shirt, sweats,
Retro J's, sounds about right.

But I wait in line,
Chain swinging cross on my chest,
I see women grab their purses,
And the elderly hold their breath.

Don't worry, it's me,
You not like what you see,
Fake smiles, fake laughs,
See my cross, asking do I believe.

Then I leave...
The Alarm sounds the Camaro,
No pants low, but 24's,
Oh, OK, he is one of those.

I get pulled over on side streets,
And the police ask questions,
License, registration please,
Should have been a pedestrian.

And then Monday comes,
Shirt, tie, slacks, no earrings,
Same swag, same guy,
Just taking in what life brings.

My appointments overbooked,
Students needing everything,
Making a difference, changing lives,
Others don't know a damn thing.

But, I smile…

PAINFUL SILENCE

My midnight showers begin with midnight prayers,
Asking God for forgiveness, answers,
Hoping to be interrupted by my love,
But instead I cleanse with sadness.

Naked walks to the bed,
Thinking my love would await,
Hoping for no need to dress,
Hearing midnight breaths… guess I'm too late.

Laying down no late night kisses,
No wands caressing my soul,
Passionate kisses becoming dreams,
Love until sunset, will I ever know?

Maybe I'll dream of you,
Make love in my deepest phase,
Warm linens, no moisture,
Awakening to the good morning rays.

No good morning my love,
Instead, we dress, to part ways,
No good bye kisses or miss you,
But, I love you and have a good day.

Miserable departures, painful returns,
Wishing that I could rip off your clothes,
But instead… busy schedules, brief cases,
Madly in love, who knows?

What's happened to us my love?
Will the fire be ignited?
This fountain is running over with words,
Heart flooded from the painful silence.

PLAYING POKER

It seems that every day begins with a battle,
And I wonder… why is life like this?
Something has to change, it has to,
I cannot continue like this.

My confidence is terrible,
And my self-esteem is shot to hell,
It's like my pride has been arrested,
And my skills and talent won't make bail.

What should I do?
Where do I go from here?
I'm praying asking God for answers,
And I'm losing this battle with fear.

My funds are low,
My certifications are limited,
Should I just end it all, give up,
I'm sure no one would miss it.

Well God, I'm going to try something new,
I'm going to step out and take risks,
Trust in you, seek guidance,
No more time to reminisce.

I have to believe in my passion,
I cannot let this napkin unfold,
Pushing my pencil across the pad,
And letting you take control.

Father God, I thank you,
Was lost, but I think that I'm found,
I took a risk and submitted my work,
And someone said that my work was profound.

Really? My work,
How could this be possible?
Can I afford this risk? Take the chance,
Should I add some more obstacles?

No need to bluff,
I have crawled the longest yards,
No need to pluck, no need to shuffle,
I'm gambling all of my cards.

I have to take the risk,
Even if I'm homeless.

RETRO J'S

When I was a kid I had a dream,
I had a dream of being on Oprah,
And my heart just showed it, all the way down to the specifics,
Nice shirt, nice pants, retro J's,
And they were definitely authentics.

It's amazing how some people dream,
And then allow the dream to fade away,
But… this dream showed me the blue print,
So I must make it happen, a focused mind, retro J's… retro 4 cements.

See this dream isn't going to dry up like a raisin in the sun,
Cause I believe that I can be the next Langston Hughes,
I have to keep believing, keep grinding, keep striving,
A tainted mind, no this dream is not going to be confused.

Cause I understand this,
I mean I got this, this tool I am going to use,
Off the top of the dome,
No pad, no pencil,
Man that boy is lighting that fuse.

Grey true religions, green shirt rocking that Mexican Flag,
Boy I feel like a "G"
That nice green, that splash of red,
Looking at my feet, retro spizike O'G's.

Yes sir, Yes sir

And I'm going to keep working,
Conversing with Oprah is where I belong,
Discussing my mind, discussing my work,
Retro J's… let's call them October's very own.

So I'm going to continue rocking these retro J's,
Because I have to live out this dream,
The dream gave me all of the specifics,
Looking down at my feet to see the retro J's,
Because the dream began with the authentics.

RITES OF PASSAGE

It's amazing how we had powerful black leaders,
Who fought for our rights, prosperity,
Martin Luther King's, "I Have a Dream,"
What message did this dream carry?

So many years of slavery,
No means of communication,
Life on the line for acquiring knowledge,
Fighting for equality, breaking segregation.

So why put ourselves in bondage,
Have skills that become useless,
Not utilizing our sources,
Being methodical and making excuses.

What happened to the dream?
What happened to the determination?
Resources are feeling the rooms,
But we are thinking evacuation.

We are attending institutions to mingle,
Hitting the clubs, learning to dance,
Sleeping in class or not attending,
But receive perfect scores in romance.

Approaching our sisters negatively,
Complimenting ladies without clothes,
Using derogatory terms on our sisters,
And the sisters responding to bitches and hoes.

Not wanting to fight for our country,
Saying the world doesn't love the brother,
But selling drugs to families and mothers,
Target practice, from killing each other.

It's seems every week someone dies,
And the young ones seem to pass,
White man kills a black man we riot,
Blacks kills blacks, do they get a pass?

Why are we not educating our kids?
Instead of just relying on schools,
Why are we cursing out our kids?
Instead of providing educational tools.

Are we the fools,
Finding ways to manipulate the system,
Selling dope in front of our kids,
Negativity comes then play the victim.

Why not stick together,
Strength does come in numbers,
But we pull each other down instead,
Hurting one another, I wonder.

We have to do better,
We have to have other remedies,
More foreign businesses,
And they are in the black communities.

RITES OF PASSAGE-CONTINUED

Someone black getting murdered,
If the suspect is white, we wanna knowing something,
But thirty eyes can see black-on-black,
But no one saw nothing.

We have to make change,
It has to start with you and me,
People we are losing our future,
Destroying our communities.

RUGGED LIONS

MANY question our capabilities,
MANY question our articulation,
MANY question our knowledge,
Frowning at our pigmentation.

SOME envy our character,
SOME doubt our progress,
SOME question our demeanor,
Wanting us to feel oppressed.

FEW trust our judgment,
FEW acknowledge our presence,
FEW believe the walking testimony,
Denying God's reflection.

NO ONE believes that it's possible,
NO ONE give credit where credit is due,
NO ONE respects the change,
Denying that the problem is… YOU!

WE ARE CUT FROM A DIFFERENT CLOTH!
We are not a resemblance of fools,
Our image is of the almighty,
It's not a resemblance of YOU.

TAINTED PICASSO'S

Father God…
I have never seen anything so chaotic,
Seeing the true meaning of divide, conquer,
Weak destroying the weak; strong destroying the strong
Kings crossing out kings with insecurities,
Powerless, fighting battles without armor.

It's been chaotic for a while now,
Kings wearing masks, swinging swords,
Having conflicted battles with the unseen,
It seems this body of water is ever ending,
From the bodies to great lakes, to forming powerless streams.
And then things turn veneer…

Do you see the picture?
The world is constantly evolving with art,
A world filled with tainted Picasso's,
Contaminated oils, diluted spirits,
A new acrylic that's not water-soluble.
Father God, I am so confused!

Who is painting these pictures?
Do you see the tainted Picasso's!?
A chaotic world with preconceived notions…
Righteous souls, bodies of water,
Authentic paints, abstract emotions.
We need some help!!

THE 3RD EYE

How deep is your psychological significance?
Have you ever made the connection?
Connection to higher consciousness',
The connection, which provides perception.

We spend a lifetime dissecting other possibilities,
Other characteristics and the nature of potential companies,
Becoming inebriated from the flattery of tongues.
Falling deeply in love with misunderstanding.

We are intrigued by the misconceptions,
Consistently seeking taking chances, and more chances,
Being afraid to perceive the unconscious,
Then being damaged by unforeseen circumstances.

Will we be released from captivity?
Becoming fully aware of the connection,
Knowing that destruction is our lack of wisdom,
And failure in the crevices of your reflection.

How deep is your psychological significance?
Are we knowledgeable of the inner self?
The key ingredient is your freedom,
And we must be saved from ourselves.

THANK YOU

Father God, I thank you,

I thank you for blessing me,
With skills, talents, abilities,
They are used to show versatility,
But to serve you, most importantly.

Thank you, for hearing my cries,
And continuing to bless me, time after time,
Increasing my wisdom, creativity,
Giving me the opportunity to express myself in between lines.

I understand that my gift has expanded,
And with this, there are no boundaries,
My work has been based upon my thoughts,
Allowing my passion to pour out of me.

My passion doesn't have room for fear,
Just expressing things in my unique way,
My goal is to speak to a diverse audience,
And say things, that many are afraid to say.

I apologize if I offended anyone,
My intentions were not to inflict pain,
I had to work from dark places,
And allow people to love and appreciate art,
As I write through my pain.

So allow me to continue Father,
As I express my passion in between lines,
I promise to bring creativity with passion,
And spark flames one poem at a time.

In Jesus' name I pray.

Amen

THE CHASE

Restrictions compliment limitations,
Limitations make love to fears,
Fears penetrate passion,
Altering paths, no time for veneer.

Procrastination compliments hindrance,
Hindrance flirts with deprive,
Deprive withholds information,
Creating bondage, keep the passion inside.

Hopes dilute dreams,
Dreams entertain passion,
Passion entertains the ego,
But do we have willingness to make it happen.

THE RELEASE

My vision becomes very blurry,
And my mind is like a door has been closed,
It's like releasing harmful chemicals,
Not knowing what poisons have been exposed.

Everything around me seems fragile,
And my hands seem as heavy as stone,
And I am so anxious to strike anything,
Because in my mind these poisons roam.

My head aches from all the distractions,
And my body just tingles from anxiety,
I know that I need to release the tension,
Because my blood boils with intensity.

I feel that I need to escape the tension,
But my mind is cluttered with frustrations,
Leaving me anxious and helpless,
So every negative aspect becomes temptation.

What am I supposed to do?
I cannot handle this pain from within,
I know that I need some kind of peace,
Before my heart and soul mends.

THE CONTRADICTION

Why are we so methodical?
Expecting the rules to be followed,
But rules are made to be broken,
And today must be forgotten tomorrow.

Does everyone receive a fair chance?
Make mistakes, ask for forgiveness,
And then move comfortable through life,
Without stress and criticism.

It seems that the congregation can be wrong,
Make mistakes and reveal them,
And then if a pastor does something wrong,
People tend to get into their feelings.

Does a pastor supposed to be perfect?
Making every move with precision,
Has a disagreement with the spouse,
Openly, now you question the vision.

Should a pastor forget about their lives?
Just sit home, pray, and read,
Give up football on Sunday's,
Just to prove that they believe.

We all have our share of troubles,
And we all need protection, guidance,
But if the pastor has been divorced,
We question whether we could confide in.

C'mon people,
I'm not trying be rude, I know that some feel that I'm wrong,
But all of our pockets should be empty,
But somehow we find a few stones.

We all know right from wrong,
And we all tend to backslide,
We have sex that's not pure,
Then call it love, better hide.

We can hit the club on Saturdays,
Take a few shots on the nightcap,
Lead the praise team on Sunday's,
Catch the spirit and run some Laps.

I just think that we should be fair,
Don't frown upon imperfection,
Because we all need guidance,
There is only one that has perfected it.

And it's not us nor the Pastor.
Just relax.

THE DOCTOR VISIT

Awakened by headaches,
Man this pain is more than I can bare,
This pain has caused numbness,
What's going on? Is my heart prepared.

I have had this same point of view,
And I was pleased with the duration,
But I have reached the end of the road,
And this requires an examination.

I have made unwarranted decisions,
Thrown pebbles in my own path,
Embracing my shortcomings,
And not appreciating my craft.

My skills and abilities require precision,
But my perspective has a unique glare,
We have once spoke on blurred vision,
But we agreed that the perception was fair.

Must I settle for less?
Shouldn't I exceed expectations?
Stretch my arms out to thee,
And allow the alterations.

Father God, I am stretched,
Please align my path,
Please guide and direct me,
I need two sets of prints in this path.

Through you all things are possible,
I am aware this may take minutes or hours,
Remove this pain, correct my vision,
I need a new prescription, increase the power.

The tough times have been evident,
Acknowledge my conviction,
Provide the answers, set me free,
Lord, please change my prescription.

A new way of life,
A different walk, a different path,
No unbearable pains,
No rocks in my path.

Father, you have all the tools,
And you enhance my skills and abilities,
My perception has been a hindrance,
Now my ideas are possibilities.

Thanks Doc.

THE JOY OF BEING USED

Why are people so afraid of being used?
Is it really that detrimental?
Being used is a part of life,
Just appreciate the fundamentals.

Let me explain...

As men, we all have been used,
Especially being involved with a beautiful girl,
And then beautiful girls dislike your beautiful girl,
So envious ones use the man,
Revealing more than diamonds and pearls.

Gotta be careful fellas...

But it doesn't stop there,
We get used at our professions,
People manipulating the system,
Trying to pull rank because they can,
Man... people sure know how to take advantage
of the system.

Some of your friends lie to you,
Make you believe they are genuine,
Being around you for the appeal,
Knowing that your swag gets them noticed,
Then you express ideas for them to steal.

Open your eyes people.
The devil uses as well,
Trying to take control,
Manipulate your life,
If he cannot get through to you,
He might just go through your wife.

See he's not this fairy tale,
Dressed up with red, wearing a pitch fork,
He is smooth, with the finest jewels,
Watch out he will send the storm,
So, he can comfort you at the airport.

We also give ourselves away,
So the lord can use us,
But this to me is a beautiful thing,
Troubles will come your way,
From all the greatness that he can bring.

So don't be afraid of being used,
Just be aware of the service,
Raise a caution flag, if you're not being used,
Because you might not be worth the service.

THE LAST DANCE

Man... Man... Man...
It has been an amazing ride,
Running out of gas to fill up,
Then running out of gas to fill up,
Having obstacles to and fro,
Traveling a road that no one knows,
But we ride...

Saying that we going to ride to the end,
But really there is no end,
Because in my mind and flesh we coincide,
Inhaling the earth to ease our minds,
Smelling her white flowers to get a rise,
So that our weakness is no longer visible,
And forever my manhood will rise...

Saying that I love you very softly,
Stroking your hair while I kiss you,
You saying please don't let go,
So with my mouth I undress you,
Tears falling while our heart beat...
Beat to the same drum, while my lower half...
Is still numb...

You feel like everything that I want,
You feel like everything that I need,
But is it because you...
Make me scream when you on your knees,
Call me "Daddy" when I'm in between,
Fuck me long and hard is what you sing,
Stroking my ego is what it seems...

Wow!!
It's been an amazing ride,
The joy of making you cum one last time,
Twirling your hair while we lie,
Kissing your lips while we cry…
Asking me for more while we dress,
Asking me for more as we smile…
So I say, until next time…

If there is a next time…
This is the last dance…

THE LAST OF A DYING BREED

I once heard that…
In order to be the image of something,
You must be in the image of something,
But, what is that something??

What if you don't understand?
Lacking the vision in order to identify,
Although there are many images of you,
And all of you have watery eyes.

Growing up fatherless…
Then mimicking fatherless soldiers,
Trying to maneuver through life,
Being constantly damaged by vultures.

Sometimes, I cannot wrap my mind around…
Damn… how does this keep… how does…
This keep evolving, taking place, happening?…
Man, its so crazy cause no one knows…

Fatherless men mimicking fatherless men,
Moving around obstacles trying not to sin,
But you don't know what you don't know,
So to sin becomes the beginning… and the end.

I don't even know where to begin…
It seems that all my contacts bring me pain,
And everyone continues to tug and pull on my name,
Sometimes, I just feel insane.

Repetitive actions expecting different,
Nothing changing, loving through my pain,
Wanting me to open up to you,
But… you cannot handle the rain.

The bottled up pain exciting the system,
Trying to stay strong for this one… and this one,
I cannot identify, they cannot identify,
So, they become blinded mistaken it for wisdom.

I wish that I could see what they see,
Because this pain gets the best of me,
I try to avoid the misery because,
I cannot let it get the best of me.

Changing up my haircuts trying to change the image,
Lying to myself manipulating myself, why me?
Crying when I see young men, praying…
Praying that I don't see a little me.

I have to find answers… I have to,
I cannot bare this pain, I swear,
Not even Clorox, Shout, or Oxy power,
Can remove this stain.

Somehow, someway this has to change,
It has to start with me,
Being a model, being a father to the fatherless,
In the image of something I have never seen.

THE LAST OF A DYING BREED-CONTINUED

Christ, I want this!!! I give it all to you!!!
I need you to plant that seed,
So, I can be the last of the fatherless,
The last of a dying breed!!

Let's take that walk!

THROUGH THE EYES OF A SINNER

I lift my head with red eyes,
Dark hood during night skies,
Damp skin from long cries,
Having deep pain in the archives.

But, it still lives, it's hungry,
Needing to find the next feast,
A new octane, fuel the beast,
Untamable, must have a leash.

But, I'm loose, no chains,
Busted knuckles from the game,
Hearing voices from my conscience,
Inspiration to my veins.

I love the smell of fear as blood boils,
Trigger fingers no recoil,
Release the fire, let it burn,
Catching lives, what are they running for?

I'm untamable.
Just another menace to society,
Not the man that I strive to be,
No options, being restricted by society.

I have no other options.

PHONE SEX

Your ringtone is so soothing,
The anticipation of hearing your tone,
Wanting to play? Try something new,
Well… let's play a little over the phone.

Don't be afraid my love,
Take your time, be free,
I'm not going to judge your words,
The sound of you impressing me…

So… after you my love,
Say your words, I will follow,
A new experience with you my love,
And then we will pick up tomorrow.

Let me help you,
What can I do with your body?

You can see it, touch it, taste it, explore it;
All you want cause baby it's yours,
No one else can even dream about touching my curves,
Like a winding road leading to that special place, my road leads straight to you. Never getting off path…

That's beautiful babe!

I love traveling your winding roads,
Roads of no return,
Kissing your lips, rubbing those hips,
Igniting my fire, just let it burn.

Let it burn babe… and let the others dream… traveling your roads… taking my time… sipping your sweetest stream.

Your turn babe… you can do it…

Stream so sweet Willy Wonka would invest; dripping of sweet nectar all down your chest. Your face buried between my thighs, only you can give me such a rise. As your tongue strokes my sweet center, my body experiences an uncontrollable quiver.

Umm…

Sweet nectar all down my chest,
Climbing walls, no need to rest,
Your secret place I want to rest… even Baloo tried to mess.

Even he needed help,
But no manipulation necessary,
Creating our April Jungle Book,
Making love, the 14th of February.

After you…

Climbing the walls of a water fall… pooling onto the sheets. Yes, no, yes, no, I tango with reaching my peak. I finally give in as my back arches off the bed. The sheets gather in my fist from this super cum. It feels so good as juices run.

Your juices run… my juices flow,

PHONE SEX-CONTINUED

Swimming the streams we go,
Yes, no, yes, no… playing tango my love, until our
bodies lose control.

That was fun babe,
Good night my love,
Good night babe, I love you more.

WHAT ARE YOU?

The slave is a man being someone's property,
His actions being controlled as well as his thoughts,
The situation can be changed with knowledge,
But his lack of knowing makes him bought.

The enslaved is a man being someone's property,
His actions controlled as well as his visions,
The situation can be changed with time,
Cause being enslaved is a condition.

The nigger is the man that has control,
And he blames the white man for his negative actions,
He makes his own excuses for his struggle,
But not knowing he is still captive.

The black man is his own property,
And he is too educated to be a slave or a nigger,
He controls his world and everything in it,
And this makes him inferior.

What are you? I am not a black man,
Because I placed myself beneath inferior,
I failed everyone including myself,
So I apologize for being a slave, I apologize for being a nigger.

THE REVENGE

I dream of nights like this,
Crescent moon, perfect silence,
Midnight sighs, midnight cries,
No regrets when the night ends.

Black shirt, black pants,
Black gloves, black mask,
Several shots of Ciroc,
Just to help the sorrows pass.

And then Mary Jane fills the air,
Let her move, let her dance,
Lift her skirt high, very high,
Our own personal romance.

No shades,
No need to hide low, red eyes,
The devil erupting in my spirit,
I have to semi-auto until sunrise.

If I do not return,
It is what it is, I have peace,
I am taking everything that was taking from me,
Who cares about rest in peace.

FORBIDDEN MESSAGES

Our lifetime consist of messages,
Messages that we reject or receive,
Every message serves its purpose,
But you decide what to believe.

You also decide how to respond,
The messages inflict change I suppose,
From frustration, to exotic moments,
Whatever it takes to remove the clothes.

Or better yet, motivate you to move,
Forcing you to seek passion,
Removing the chains from your mind,
Heart palpitations no distractions.

Yessir

Distractions must be removed,
Re-shifting your focus to precede,
Not changing clothes for 144 hours,
Removing life's choke hold, just breathe.

Just breathe…
Breathe, and don't be afraid to listen,
Wisdom is not background music,
And forbidden messages are premonitions.

AFRICAN DIAMONDS

Are we aware of the diamond trade?
The civil wars, lives being lost,
Seeking something in its purity,
Destroying countries by any cost...

Genocide, for the purest pieces,
Mischievous flirting with egregious,
Playing God for possessions,
Manipulation for precious secrets.

Are we aware of the diamond trade?
The reinvented barter system,
Manipulation for previous secrets,
Taking advantage tainted images.

Does the diamond trade still exist?
Fighting battles, losing souls,
Men manipulating our sisters,
Destroying lives, as the day unfolds.

Putting marks on their portrait,
Corrupted mines, calling it passion,
Telling lies beneath the sheets,
Denying that vandalism never happened.

Our sisters are African Diamonds,
In the purest form, know your worth,
Your creation is profound,
Only you can populate the Earth.

Hair filled with strength,
Lips filled with passion,
Eyes that light up the evening,
Hips that can cause distractions.

Touch so significant,
Complexion shining like pearls,
Your presence is one of a kind,
Intelligence out of this world…

So you must be appreciated,
Beautiful diamonds, no need to bluff,
Walking diamonds, throughout the world,
Deepest secrets, where is the rough?

Please… understand your purpose,
Your significance is so divine,
Don't conform, never settle,
Secrets found deep within the mines.

Our African Diamonds…

BLINDFOLDS

It seems that every decision I make is wrong,
Arguing about that and this, this and that,
Reminiscing about my previous flings,
Wondering if I should bring my old thing back.

I wanted to bury that old me,
Move on to greater things, be better,
Making sacrifices for my family, my queen,
But I find myself writing midnight letters.

No letters to you,
But contemplating my thoughts, next moves,
Trying to find ways to provide stability,
We argue, and then I ponder the next groove.

I'm tired of discussing scandals,
And these unforgettable persuasions,
You complain about my grind and time,
But these scandals say I'm amazing.

I'm so confused.

I work my ass off to receive better,
Because you and I want more,
But, you argue over time and leisure,
But, leisure doesn't pay bills, what are we fighting for?

I apologize for wanting success,
I apologize for trying to give you the best,
Never had these problems being broke,
Being a gentleman is too much stress.

We take day trips from your purse,
Adding petroleum to your cars,
Pay the bills with your sweat,
To only complain about tomorrow.

I once dreamed of covering it all,
Freeing us both from the hard-work,
I believe that my vision could be the answer,
But my efforts seem to make things worse.

I have seen women work hard,
Their men staying at home,
Dropping the women off to work,
Taking her car to roam.

I have seen women take men shopping, improving his swag,
This cycle is insane,
Having no means to be better,
Sitting home with video games.

Don't worry, I understand now,
No need to pursue the dream,
I must cover my eyes with the blindfold,
And drown in the powerful streams.

FLESH WARS

You're looking very sexy over there in that dress,
Let me guess, is it Prada?
I once heard stories of you falling from the heavens,
Right after everything went sour.

But... you are here now,
One third of the heavens wasn't enough,
Causing so many problems for these fellas,
Breaking up homes... girl you tough.

You have the power to alter minds,
Which can throw off a man's spirit,
The Lord told me to look out for it,
Guess I should have taken it more serious.

I remember when I was with ol' girl,
Moving steady, possibly becoming serious,
You came out of nowhere with sweet nothings,
Game so smooth, I just had to experience.

Even when I tried to ignore you,
I knew all my weaknesses were tests,
You had a way to alter my mind,
Not moving by spirit, but moving by flesh.

Man, I just felt so bad,
Too good to be true it seems,
That smile, them hips, that voice,
You were even affecting my dreams.

It was so heavy, so heavy,
In my dreams I couldn't resist it,
Then I would wake up angry looking for you,
Because the dreams seemed so realistic.

All my cravings were answered, it's crazy,
I didn't want stress by any means,
Then out of nowhere my friends would pop up,
Box of cigars, smelling the earth through the jeans.

For you, I would inhale for good measure,
I needed it to get me through,
Just in case we had a long night, you know…
Cannot get too excited with you.

That smile, them hips, that voice,
I'm constantly losing my focus with you,
I was told that I could be anything,
As long as I didn't fool with you.

But you are so convincing,
You make promises and then you trick me,
Looking so sexy causing problems,
I promise you are out to get me.

That smile, them hips, that voice,
One last dance, one more taste,
I need to be moved spiritually,
You control me above and below the waist.

FLESH WARS-CONTINUED

    Maybe not... I believe it's time,
    I need to resist, flee, just run,
    You have been controlling for too long,
    Your youth, the flattery of your tongue.

    This flesh war is so dangerous,
    I have to let go, be set free,
    This amazing ride has been fun,
    But, know this is not for me.

TUG OF WAR

Sometimes I pray for peaceful moments,
Asking God to cover me with his anointing,
Protection from vultures… vultures,
Praying on my conscience.

Nibbling at my mind, surrounding…
Changing perspectives, making me believe,
Going against the grain with emotions,
Damaged waves, as the sand recedes.

But I proceed… Yes, I proceed,
Asking God… Please! Cover me with your anointing,
An altered vision, Purple Heart,
Patchy skin, where is the ointment?

Hmm!! What did I pray for previously?
I feel like there is something missing,
Praying for covering, but feeling naked,
Nostalgic moments… premonitions.

My conflicted mind searches for more,
Believing that something awaits,
A corrected vision, peaceful moments,
Help me God!! For my sake…

PERFECT IMPERFECTION

Baby! What happened to us?
We were so deep in love,
Sharing last names before marriage,
Dreaming of throwing rice, white turtledoves.

I remember when we couldn't wait…
To get off from work to call each other,
Going to bed with conversation,
Just so we could dream of one another.

Now we are divided in our home,
Going to work without conversation,
Not looking forward to returning home,
Place of peace without relaxation.

It's like we are strangers,
And I'm not ready to receive it,
We made love the other night,
And I felt like I cheated.

Our love is no longer present,
Too much pride for forgiveness,
Zero support, no desire to lead,
No need to support the vision.

What do I need to do my love?
No need to point fingers,
No need to destroy the home,
Because that foul smell will linger.

It's not about me!
I am willing to bare the pain,
I am willing to weather any storm,
But can we handle the rain?

I am not perfect babe!
Neither are you!
But isn't this worth fighting for?
I will get in the ring with you.

All I want is our love,
I miss our connection,
Neither one of us are perfect babe,
Let's correct the perfect imperfections.

I REMEMBER

I remember! Do you remember?

Tag you it,
Hide and seek,
Training wheels to Big Wheels,
Halloween, Trick-or-Treat.

RC Colas,
Nehi Peach,
Cracker Jacks,
No Swisher Sweets.

Duck, Duck, Goose,
Slamming screen doors,
Sleep-overs, quarter waters,
Camp fires, making S'mores.

I remember! Do you remember?

Hand-me-downs,
That would never last,
Pro Keds, LA Gears,
Bugle Boys and Jordache.

The Electric Slide,
The Boogie Woogie,
Sugar Mamas, Sugar Daddy's,
Snotty nose, playing hooky.

Five dollar haircuts,
New era, wearing cross colors,
Grandmothers in their sixties,
Same fathers, same mothers.

I remember! Do you remember?

Drama free,
No locked doors,
Old stories, appreciated wisdom,
Dr. King, what a beautiful dream.

Relationships, chivalry,
Appreciation for mankind,
Construction workers, building blocks,
New beginnings, so divine.

Beautiful cities,
Powerful streams,
Technology in motion,
Colorful dreams.

I remember! Do you remember?

THE PURSUIT OF HAPPINESS

What is the pursuit of happiness?
Do you have a complete understanding of happiness?
I understand if your mind is boggled by pessimistic views,
Altering your perspective and filling your heart with sadness.

It's okay; many people misconstrue sadness with happiness,
Settling with short-comings and their mistakes,
Accepting failures and lacking ambition,
Wearing their happy mask and continuing to perpetuate.

What is the pursuit of happiness?
Do you have a complete understanding of happiness?
I understand if your belief is another persons' vision,
Causing you to dance with bewilderment.

It's okay; many people misconstrue vision with blindness,
Traveling down wicked roads relying on hindsight,
Being irritated from the misconception,
Because you are wearing a blindfold at midnight.

What is the pursuit of happiness?
Do you have a complete understanding of happiness?
I understand if you are afraid of the risks,
Causing you to create boundaries, constructing your hindrance.

It's okay; many people misconstrue settlement with sabotage,
Having comfort zones with limitations,
Not having the desire in making the impossible possible,
Because your failure is equivalent to relaxation.

ABOUT THE AUTHOR

Hello readers, my name is Kenneth A. Brown, Jr. and I am originally from Lenoir, NC, but was raised in Marion, NC. I have experienced my fair share of adversity; however, I do not use this as an excuse to not pursue my dreams. I received a Bachelors Degree in English from Winston-Salem State University and pursuing a Masters degree in School Counseling from North Carolina A&T State University. I believe that every person should be different and develop a sense of comfort with that difference. Poetry forces my mind to constantly run and generate thoughts, which I expressed without using a filter. With my work, I hope to spark conversations filled with deep thought, controversy, or simply allow individuals to view things through a different lens. So, I entitled this book "My Thoughts, Through the Eyes of a Sinner." I am not perfect by any means and all of these poems were written to illustrate my consistent struggles in life, but also discuss thoughts and ideas from multiple perspectives. I believe that we all have struggles of some sort and I find it intriguing to write about situations without any fear. I hope that each reader can find a poem that is relatable and have as much fun as I did creating the work.

Thank you.